Meditating on the Sorrowful Mysteries

An Intentional Rosary

Amy Schisler

Bozman, MD 2023

Copyright 2023 by Amy Schisler

Chesapeake Sunrise Publishing

ISBN: 979-8-9883677-9-6

Published by:
Chesapeake Sunrise Publishing
Amy Schisler
Bozman, MD
2023

$\mathcal{T}$able of Contents

$\mathcal{H}$ow to use this book

An intentional Rosary is said with a pause before each Hail Mary within the five decades of the Rosary. This pause enables you to insert your own petition or to pray for the needs or prayer requests of others. The petitions in this book are inserted so you may meditate more deeply on the Sorrowful Mysteries. You may follow the prayers included, or you may substitute your own prayers. A favorite prayer of mine is The Memorare. I always close my Rosary with this prayer. I have included it at the end of the Rosary for your use.

May our Blessed Mother and her Son bestow upon you many blessings as you follow her request to pray the Rosary.

From the United States Conference of Catholic Bishops:
The Rosary is a Scripture-based prayer. It begins with the Apostles' Creed, which summarizes the great mysteries of the Catholic faith. The Our

Father, which introduces each mystery, is from the Gospels. The first part of the Hail Mary is the angel's words announcing Christ's birth and Elizabeth's greeting to Mary. St. Pius V officially added the second part of the Hail Mary. The Mysteries of the Rosary center on the events of Christ's life. There are four sets of Mysteries: Sorrowful , Sorrowful, Sorrowful and—added by Saint John Paul II in 2002—the Luminous.

Typical Days to Pray Each Rosary:
Sunday and Wednesday – Glorious
Monday and Saturday – Joyful
Tuesday and Friday – Sorrowful
Thursday – Luminous

The Beginning of the Rosary

In the Name of the Father, and of the Son, and of the Holy Spirit. Amen

I believe in God,
the Father almighty,
Creator of heaven and earth,
and in Jesus Christ, his only Son, our Lord,
who was conceived by the Holy Spirit,
born of the Virgin Mary,
suffered under Pontius Pilate,
was crucified, died and was buried;
he descended into hell;
on the third day he rose again from the dead;
he ascended into heaven,
and is seated at the right hand of God the Father almighty;
from there he will come to judge the living and the dead.
I believe in the Holy Spirit,
the holy catholic Church,
the communion of saints,
the forgiveness of sins,

the resurrection of the body,
and life everlasting.
Amen.

Our Father, who art in Heaven, hallowed
be thy name.
Thy kingdom come.
Thy will be done on Earth as it is in
Heaven.
Give us this day our daily bread,
And forgive us our trespasses as we
forgive those who trespass against us.
And lead us not into temptation, but
deliver us from evil.
Amen

For the grace of Faith:
Hail Mary, full of grace.
The Lord is with thee.
Blessed art thou among women,
And blessed is the fruit of thy womb,
Jesus.
Holy Mary, Mother of God,
Pray for us sinners,
Now and at the hour of death.
Amen

For the grace of Hope:
Hail Mary, full of grace.
The Lord is with thee.
Blessed art thou among women,
And blessed is the fruit of thy womb,
Jesus.
Holy Mary, Mother of God,
Pray for us sinners,
Now and at the hour of death.
Amen

For the grace of Charity:
Hail Mary, full of grace.
The Lord is with thee.
Blessed art thou among women,
And blessed is the fruit of thy womb,
Jesus.
Holy Mary, Mother of God,
Pray for us sinners,
Now and at the hour of death.
Amen

Glory be to the Father,
And the Son,
And the Holy Spirit,
As now and ever shall be,
World without end.
Amen

*T*he First Sorrowful Mystery:

The Agony in the Garden
Matthew 26:36-46

Then Jesus came with them to a place called Gethsemane, and he said to his disciples, "Sit here while I go over there and pray." He took along Peter and the two sons of Zebedee, and began to feel sorrow and distress. Then he said to them, "My soul is sorrowful even to death. Remain here and keep watch with me."

He advanced a little and fell prostrate in prayer, saying, "My Father, if it is possible, let this cup pass from me; yet, not as I will, but as you will."

When he returned to his disciples he found them asleep. He said to Peter, "So you could not keep watch with me for one hour? Watch and pray that you may not undergo the test. The spirit is willing, but the flesh is weak."

Withdrawing a second time, he prayed again, "My Father, if it is not possible that this cup pass without my drinking it, your will be done!"

Then he returned once more and found them asleep, for they could not keep their eyes open. He left them and withdrew again and prayed a third time, saying the same thing again. Then he returned to his disciples and said to them, "Are you still sleeping and taking your rest? Behold, the hour is at hand when the Son of Man is to be handed over to sinners. Get up, let us go. Look, my betrayer is at hand."

Our Father, who art in Heaven, hallowed be thy name.
Thy kingdom come.
Thy will be done on Earth as it is in Heaven.
Give us this day our daily bread,
And forgive us our trespasses as we forgive those who trespass against us.
And lead us not into temptation, but deliver us from evil.
Amen

That the Holy Spirit will send help to those trying to do God's will:
Hail Mary, full of grace.
The Lord is with thee.
Blessed art thou among women,

And blessed is the fruit of thy womb,
Jesus.
Holy Mary, Mother of God,
Pray for us sinners,
Now and at the hour of death.
Amen

*For those who are unable to keep God's Word,
that they will be awakened by His love:*
Hail Mary, full of grace.
The Lord is with thee.
Blessed art thou among women,
And blessed is the fruit of thy womb,
Jesus.
Holy Mary, Mother of God,
Pray for us sinners,
Now and at the hour of death.
Amen

*For those who feel sorrow and distress, that the
love of God will comfort them:*
Hail Mary, full of grace.
The Lord is with thee.
Blessed art thou among women,
And blessed is the fruit of thy womb,
Jesus.
Holy Mary, Mother of God,

Pray for us sinners,
Now and at the hour of death.
Amen

For those who keep watch over God's people:
Hail Mary, full of grace.
The Lord is with thee.
Blessed art thou among women,
And blessed is the fruit of thy womb,
Jesus.
Holy Mary, Mother of God,
Pray for us sinners,
Now and at the hour of death.
Amen

*For those praying that the cup of suffering may
pass them by:*
Hail Mary, full of grace.
The Lord is with thee.
Blessed art thou among women,
And blessed is the fruit of thy womb,
Jesus.
Holy Mary, Mother of God,
Pray for us sinners,
Now and at the hour of death.
Amen

For those who suffer with dignity, offering their pain up to God, that they will feel the hand of God upon them:

Hail Mary, full of grace.

The Lord is with thee.

Blessed art thou among women,

And blessed is the fruit of thy womb, Jesus.

Holy Mary, Mother of God,

Pray for us sinners,

Now and at the hour of death.

Amen

For those whose souls are willing but whose flesh is weak:

Hail Mary, full of grace.

The Lord is with thee.

Blessed art thou among women,

And blessed is the fruit of thy womb, Jesus.

Holy Mary, Mother of God,

Pray for us sinners,

Now and at the hour of death.

Amen

For those praying for discernment of God's Will in their lives:

Hail Mary, full of grace.
The Lord is with thee.
Blessed art thou among women,
And blessed is the fruit of thy womb,
Jesus.
Holy Mary, Mother of God,
Pray for us sinners,
Now and at the hour of death.
Amen

*That the Holy Spirit will reveal to me God's
Will in my life and that I may accept it:*
Hail Mary, full of grace.
The Lord is with thee.
Blessed art thou among women,
And blessed is the fruit of thy womb,
Jesus.
Holy Mary, Mother of God,
Pray for us sinners,
Now and at the hour of death.
Amen

*That those who have been betrayed will offer
forgiveness and find peace:*
Hail Mary, full of grace.
The Lord is with thee.
Blessed art thou among women,

And blessed is the fruit of thy womb,
Jesus.
Holy Mary, Mother of God,
Pray for us sinners,
Now and at the hour of death.
Amen

Glory be to the Father,
And the Son,
And the Holy Spirit,
As now and ever shall be,
World without end.
Amen

O my Jesus, forgive us our sins, save us
from the fires of hell; lead all souls to
Heaven, especially those who have most
need of your mercy.

*T*he Second Sorrowful Mystery:
The Scourging at the Pillar
Matthew 27:16-18, 20-26

And at that time they had a notorious prisoner called Barabbas. So when they had assembled, Pilate said to them, "Which one do you want me to release to you, Barabbas, or Jesus called Messiah?" For he knew that it was out of envy that they had handed him over.

The chief priests and the elders persuaded the crowds to ask for Barabbas but to destroy Jesus. The governor said to them in reply, "Which of the two do you want me to release to you?" They answered, "Barabbas!"

Pilate said to them, "Then what shall I do with Jesus called Messiah?" They all said, "Let him be crucified!" But he said, "Why? What evil has he done?" They only shouted the louder, "Let him be crucified!" When Pilate saw that he was not succeeding at all, but that a riot was breaking out instead, he took water and washed his hands in the sight of the crowd, saying, "I am innocent of this man's blood. Look to it

yourselves." And the whole people said in reply,
"His blood be upon us and upon our children."

Then he released Barabbas to them, but after he
had Jesus scourged, he handed him over to be
crucified.

Our Father, who art in Heaven, hallowed
be thy name.
Thy kingdom come.
Thy will be done on Earth as it is in
Heaven.
Give us this day our daily bread,
And forgive us our trespasses as we
forgive those who trespass against us.
And lead us not into temptation, but
deliver us from evil.
Amen

For those suffering with afflictions of the body:
Hail Mary, full of grace.
The Lord is with thee.
Blessed art thou among women,
And blessed is the fruit of thy womb,
Jesus.
Holy Mary, Mother of God,

Pray for us sinners,
Now and at the hour of death.
Amen

For those who suffer at the hands of others:
Hail Mary, full of grace.
The Lord is with thee.
Blessed art thou among women,
And blessed is the fruit of thy womb,
Jesus.
Holy Mary, Mother of God,
Pray for us sinners,
Now and at the hour of death.
Amen

That those who inflict pain on others will see the face of God in their victims and repent:
Hail Mary, full of grace.
The Lord is with thee.
Blessed art thou among women,
And blessed is the fruit of thy womb,
Jesus.
Holy Mary, Mother of God,
Pray for us sinners,
Now and at the hour of death.
Amen

For forgiveness for the times I have hurt others:
Hail Mary, full of grace.
The Lord is with thee.
Blessed art thou among women,
And blessed is the fruit of thy womb,
Jesus.
Holy Mary, Mother of God,
Pray for us sinners,
Now and at the hour of death.
Amen

For restraint from saying or doing things that cause mental or physical pain to others:
Hail Mary, full of grace.
The Lord is with thee.
Blessed art thou among women,
And blessed is the fruit of thy womb,
Jesus.
Holy Mary, Mother of God,
Pray for us sinners,
Now and at the hour of death.
Amen

For those who suffer the pain and agony of war, that they will someday live in peace:
Hail Mary, full of grace.

The Lord is with thee.
Blessed art thou among women,
And blessed is the fruit of thy womb,
Jesus.
Holy Mary, Mother of God,
Pray for us sinners,
Now and at the hour of death.
Amen

For the oppressed in the world, that they will be given justice:
Hail Mary, full of grace.
The Lord is with thee.
Blessed art thou among women,
And blessed is the fruit of thy womb,
Jesus.
Holy Mary, Mother of God,
Pray for us sinners,
Now and at the hour of death.
Amen

For those who advocate for or participate in the death of others, that they will repent and seek forgiveness:
Hail Mary, full of grace.
The Lord is with thee.
Blessed art thou among women,

And blessed is the fruit of thy womb,
Jesus.
Holy Mary, Mother of God,
Pray for us sinners,
Now and at the hour of death.
Amen

*For those who willingly take the place of others
so that someone else will be spared pain or death:*
Hail Mary, full of grace.
The Lord is with thee.
Blessed art thou among women,
And blessed is the fruit of thy womb,
Jesus.
Holy Mary, Mother of God,
Pray for us sinners,
Now and at the hour of death.
Amen

*That I will have the courage to accept suffering
and offer it in prayer to God:*
Hail Mary, full of grace.
The Lord is with thee.
Blessed art thou among women,
And blessed is the fruit of thy womb,
Jesus.

Holy Mary, Mother of God,
Pray for us sinners,
Now and at the hour of death.
Amen

Glory be to the Father,
And the Son,
And the Holy Spirit,
As now and ever shall be,
World without end.
Amen

O my Jesus, forgive us our sins, save us
from the fires of hell; lead all souls to
Heaven, especially those who have most
need of your mercy.

*T*he Third Sorrowful Mystery:
The Crowning With Thorns
Matthew 27:27-31

Then the soldiers of the governor took Jesus inside the praetorium and gathered the whole cohort around him. They stripped off his clothes and threw a scarlet military cloak about him.

Weaving a crown out of thorns, they placed it on his head, and a reed in his right hand. And kneeling before him, they mocked him, saying, "Hail, King of the Jews!"

They spat upon him and took the reed and kept striking him on the head. And when they had mocked him, they stripped him of the cloak, dressed him in his own clothes, and led him off to crucify him.

Our Father, who art in Heaven, hallowed be thy name.
Thy kingdom come.
Thy will be done on Earth as it is in Heaven.

Give us this day our daily bread,
And forgive us our trespasses as we
forgive those who trespass against us.
And lead us not into temptation, but
deliver us from evil.
Amen

*For those who are publicly humiliated to satisfy
the gains of others:*
Hail Mary, full of grace.
The Lord is with thee.
Blessed art thou among women,
And blessed is the fruit of thy womb,
Jesus.
Holy Mary, Mother of God,
Pray for us sinners,
Now and at the hour of death.
Amen

*For wisdom and good discernment for world
leaders and those in power:*
Hail Mary, full of grace.
The Lord is with thee.
Blessed art thou among women,
And blessed is the fruit of thy womb,
Jesus.
Holy Mary, Mother of God,

Pray for us sinners,
Now and at the hour of death.
Amen

For those who are tortured for the sake of politics:
Hail Mary, full of grace.
The Lord is with thee.
Blessed art thou among women,
And blessed is the fruit of thy womb,
Jesus.
Holy Mary, Mother of God,
Pray for us sinners,
Now and at the hour of death.
Amen

For those in the military and police forces, that they will seek the will of God as they carry out their duties.
Hail Mary, full of grace.
The Lord is with thee.
Blessed art thou among women,
And blessed is the fruit of thy womb,
Jesus.
Holy Mary, Mother of God,
Pray for us sinners,

Now and at the hour of death.
Amen

For those who are mocked and ridiculed:
Hail Mary, full of grace.
The Lord is with thee.
Blessed art thou among women,
And blessed is the fruit of thy womb,
Jesus.
Holy Mary, Mother of God,
Pray for us sinners,
Now and at the hour of death.
Amen

For a spiritual awakening for those who mock God and His teachings:
Hail Mary, full of grace.
The Lord is with thee.
Blessed art thou among women,
And blessed is the fruit of thy womb,
Jesus.
Holy Mary, Mother of God,
Pray for us sinners,
Now and at the hour of death.
Amen

For the innocent who are condemned to death:

Hail Mary, full of grace.
The Lord is with thee.
Blessed art thou among women,
And blessed is the fruit of thy womb,
Jesus.
Holy Mary, Mother of God,
Pray for us sinners,
Now and at the hour of death.
Amen

For removal of the thorns in my life that are causing me pain:
Hail Mary, full of grace.
The Lord is with thee.
Blessed art thou among women,
And blessed is the fruit of thy womb,
Jesus.
Holy Mary, Mother of God,
Pray for us sinners,
Now and at the hour of death.
Amen

For forgiveness for the times I have stripped others of their dignity and humanity:
Hail Mary, full of grace.
The Lord is with thee.

Jesus.
Holy Mary, Mother of God,
Pray for us sinners,
Now and at the hour of death.
Amen

*That all have faith that the Lord's promises to
His people will be fulfilled:*
Hail Mary, full of grace.
The Lord is with thee.
Blessed art thou among women,
And blessed is the fruit of thy womb,
Jesus.
Holy Mary, Mother of God,
Pray for us sinners,
Now and at the hour of death.
Amen

*That all the faithful will be filled with the desire
to strive for ongoing conversion:*
Hail Mary, full of grace.
The Lord is with thee.
Blessed art thou among women,
And blessed is the fruit of thy womb,
Jesus.
Holy Mary, Mother of God,
Pray for us sinners,

Now and at the hour of death.
Amen

Glory be to the Father,
And the Son,
And the Holy Spirit,
As now and ever shall be,
World without end.
Amen

O my Jesus, forgive us our sins, save us
from the fires of hell; lead all souls to
Heaven, especially those who have most
need of your mercy.

*T*he Fourth Luminous Mystery:
The Transfiguration
Matthew 17:1-8

After six days Jesus took Peter, James, and John his brother, and led them up a high mountain by themselves. And he was transfigured before them; his face shone like the sun and his clothes became white as light. And behold, Moses and Elijah appeared to them, conversing with him.

Then Peter said to Jesus in reply, "Lord, it is good that we are here. If you wish, I will make three tents here, one for you, one for Moses, and one for Elijah." While he was still speaking, behold, a bright cloud cast a shadow over them, then from the cloud came a voice that said, "This is my beloved Son, with whom I am well pleased; listen to him."

When the disciples heard this, they fell prostrate and were very much afraid. But Jesus came and touched them, saying, "Rise, and do not be afraid." And when the disciples raised their eyes, they saw no one else but Jesus alone.

Our Father, who art in Heaven, hallowed
be thy name.
Thy kingdom come.
Thy will be done on Earth as it is in
Heaven.
Give us this day our daily bread,
And forgive us our trespasses as we
forgive those who trespass against us.
And lead us not into temptation, but
deliver us from evil.
Amen

*That the Lord will allow us many mountaintop
moments in our lives in which we can rejoice in
God's glory:*
Hail Mary, full of grace.
The Lord is with thee.
Blessed art thou among women,
And blessed is the fruit of thy womb,
Jesus.
Holy Mary, Mother of God,
Pray for us sinners,
Now and at the hour of death.
Amen

*For those who will, on this day, look upon the
face of God in all its glory:*

Hail Mary, full of grace.
The Lord is with thee.
Blessed art thou among women,
And blessed is the fruit of thy womb,
Jesus.
Holy Mary, Mother of God,
Pray for us sinners,
Now and at the hour of death.
Amen

*That we may be made worthy to share in the
promises made to Moses and Elijah:*
Hail Mary, full of grace.
The Lord is with thee.
Blessed art thou among women,
And blessed is the fruit of thy womb,
Jesus.
Holy Mary, Mother of God,
Pray for us sinners,
Now and at the hour of death.
Amen

*For the reminder that I, too, must converse with
Jesus in my daily life:*
Hail Mary, full of grace.
The Lord is with thee.
Blessed art thou among women,

And blessed is the fruit of thy womb,
Jesus.
Holy Mary, Mother of God,
Pray for us sinners,
Now and at the hour of death.
Amen

*For those who seek shelter and a place to rest in
God's loving kindness and mercy:*
Hail Mary, full of grace.
The Lord is with thee.
Blessed art thou among women,
And blessed is the fruit of thy womb,
Jesus.
Holy Mary, Mother of God,
Pray for us sinners,
Now and at the hour of death.
Amen

*That we will always remember that we, too, are
beloved sons and daughters of God:*
Hail Mary, full of grace.
The Lord is with thee.
Blessed art thou among women,
And blessed is the fruit of thy womb,
Jesus.

Holy Mary, Mother of God,
Pray for us sinners,
Now and at the hour of death.
Amen

*That we will spend our lives striving to do what
is good and pleasing to God:*
Hail Mary, full of grace.
The Lord is with thee.
Blessed art thou among women,
And blessed is the fruit of thy womb,
Jesus.
Holy Mary, Mother of God,
Pray for us sinners,
Now and at the hour of death.
Amen

For those who live in fear:
Hail Mary, full of grace.
The Lord is with thee.
Blessed art thou among women,
And blessed is the fruit of thy womb,
Jesus.
Holy Mary, Mother of God,
Pray for us sinners,
Now and at the hour of death.
Amen

For those who find themselves alone in this world:
Hail Mary, full of grace.
The Lord is with thee.
Blessed art thou among women,
And blessed is the fruit of thy womb,
Jesus.
Holy Mary, Mother of God,
Pray for us sinners,
Now and at the hour of death.
Amen

For those who do not recognize the glory of God in their lives:
Hail Mary, full of grace.
The Lord is with thee.
Blessed art thou among women,
And blessed is the fruit of thy womb,
Jesus.
Holy Mary, Mother of God,
Pray for us sinners,
Now and at the hour of death.
Amen

Glory be to the Father,
And the Son,

And the Holy Spirit,
As now and ever shall be,
World without end.
Amen

O my Jesus, forgive us our sins, save us
from the fires of hell; lead all souls to
Heaven, especially those who have most
need of your mercy.

*T*he Fifth Luminous Mystery:
The Institution of the Eucharist
Matthew 26:26-29

While they were eating, Jesus took bread, said the blessing, broke it, and giving it to his disciples said, "Take and eat; this is my body. Then he took a cup, gave thanks, and gave it to them, saying, "Drink from it, all of you, for this is my blood of the covenant, which will be shed on behalf of many for the forgiveness of sins.

I tell you, from now on I shall not drink this fruit of the vine until the day when I drink it new with you in the kingdom of my Father."

Our Father, who art in Heaven, hallowed be thy name.
Thy kingdom come.
Thy will be done on Earth as it is in Heaven.
Give us this day our daily bread,
And forgive us our trespasses as we forgive those who trespass against us.
And lead us not into temptation, but

deliver us from evil.
Amen

That all who partake in eating the Body and drinking the Blood of Christ will be united to Christ through grace:
Hail Mary, full of grace.
The Lord is with thee.
Blessed art thou among women,
And blessed is the fruit of thy womb, Jesus.
Holy Mary, Mother of God,
Pray for us sinners,
Now and at the hour of death.
Amen

That we may be transformed, through the Eucharist, into a new being in Christ:
Hail Mary, full of grace.
The Lord is with thee.
Blessed art thou among women,
And blessed is the fruit of thy womb, Jesus.
Holy Mary, Mother of God,
Pray for us sinners,
Now and at the hour of death.
Amen

That it will be revealed to all Catholics that the Eucharist is the true Body and Blood of Christ:
Hail Mary, full of grace.
The Lord is with thee.
Blessed art thou among women,
And blessed is the fruit of thy womb, Jesus.
Holy Mary, Mother of God,
Pray for us sinners,
Now and at the hour of death.
Amen

That the rest of the world will long for the Eucharist in their lives:
Hail Mary, full of grace.
The Lord is with thee.
Blessed art thou among women,
And blessed is the fruit of thy womb, Jesus.
Holy Mary, Mother of God,
Pray for us sinners,
Now and at the hour of death.
Amen

That those seeking Christ will be led to His True Presence:

Hail Mary, full of grace.
The Lord is with thee.
Blessed art thou among women,
And blessed is the fruit of thy womb,
Jesus.
Holy Mary, Mother of God,
Pray for us sinners,
Now and at the hour of death.
Amen

For all clergy and lay ministers of the Eucharist:
Hail Mary, full of grace.
The Lord is with thee.
Blessed art thou among women,
And blessed is the fruit of thy womb,
Jesus.
Holy Mary, Mother of God,
Pray for us sinners,
Now and at the hour of death.
Amen

That we will be filled with the Holy Spirit each time we participate on the sacrifice of the Mass:
Hail Mary, full of grace.
The Lord is with thee.
Blessed art thou among women,
And blessed is the fruit of thy womb,

Jesus.
Holy Mary, Mother of God,
Pray for us sinners,
Now and at the hour of death.
Amen

*That all people come to recognize Jesus as the
Lamb of God sent from Heaven:*
Hail Mary, full of grace.
The Lord is with thee.
Blessed art thou among women,
And blessed is the fruit of thy womb,
Jesus.
Holy Mary, Mother of God,
Pray for us sinners,
Now and at the hour of death.
Amen

*That all people will discover their place at the
Supper of the Lamb:*
Hail Mary, full of grace.
The Lord is with thee.
Blessed art thou among women,
And blessed is the fruit of thy womb,
Jesus.
Holy Mary, Mother of God,

Pray for us sinners,
Now and at the hour of death.
Amen

*That I will be seated at the table of the Lamb
for all eternity:*
Hail Mary, full of grace.
The Lord is with thee.
Blessed art thou among women,
And blessed is the fruit of thy womb,
Jesus.
Holy Mary, Mother of God,
Pray for us sinners,
Now and at the hour of death.
Amen

Glory be to the Father,
And the Son,
And the Holy Spirit,
As now and ever shall be,
World without end.
Amen

O my Jesus, forgive us our sins, save us
from the fires of hell; lead all souls to
Heaven, especially those who have most
need of your mercy.

*T*he End of the Rosary

Hail, Holy Queen, Mother of Mercy,
our life, our sweetness and our hope.
To thee do we cry,
poor banished children of Eve.
To thee do we send up our sighs,
mourning and weeping in this valley of
tears.
Turn then, most gracious advocate,
thine eyes of mercy toward us,
and after this our exile
show unto us the blessed fruit of thy
womb, Jesus.
O clement, O loving,
O sweet Virgin Mary.

Pray for us, O holy Mother of God.
That we may be made worthy of the
promises of Christ

O God, whose Only Begotten Son, by
his life, Death, and Resurrection, has
purchased for us the rewards of eternal
life, grant, we beseech thee, that while

meditating on these mysteries of the most holy Rosary of the Blessed Virgin Mary, we may imitate what they contain and obtain what they promise, through the same Christ our Lord. Amen.

*T*he Memorare

Remember, O most gracious Virgin Mary, that never was it known that anyone who fled to thy protection, implored thy help, or sought thy intercession, was left unaided.

Inspired by this confidence I fly unto thee, O Virgin of virgins, my Mother.

To thee do I come, before thee I stand, sinful and Luminous.

O Mother of the Word Incarnate, despise not my petitions, but in thy mercy hear and answer me.

Amen.

In the Name of the Father, and of the Son, and of the Holy Spirit.

Amen

$\mathcal{P}$rayers and Petitions

_____

_____

_____

_____

_____

_____

_____

_____

_____

www.ingramcontent.com/pod-product-compliance
Lightning Source LLC
Chambersburg PA
CBHW020345130626
46549CB00003B/1305